CREATING A BUTTERFLY GARDEN

CREATING A BUTTERFLY GARDEN

A Guide to Attracting
and
Identifying Butterfly Visitors

by Marcus Schneck

A Fireside Book
Published by Simon & Schuster Inc.

Fireside
Simon & Schuster Building
Rockefeller Center
1230 Avenue of the Americas
New York, New York 10020

This book was designed and produced by
Quarto Publishing Inc.
The Old Brewery
6 Blundell Street
London N7 9BH

SENIOR EDITOR Sally MacEachern
COPY EDITOR Maggi McCormick
SENIOR ART EDITOR Amanda Bakhtiar
DESIGNER Sheila Volpe

ILLUSTRATORS Wayne Ford,
Paul Richardson, Sally Launder
ART DIRECTOR Moira Clinch
EDITORIAL DIRECTOR Sophie Collins
TYPESET BY Diamond Graphics
MANUFACTURED BY Eray Scan,
Singapore
PRINTED BY Leefung Asco Printers Ltd,
China

10 9 8 7

Library of Congress Cataloging in
Publication Data

Schneck, Marcus.
      Creating a butterfly garden: a
guide to attracting and identifying
butterfly visitors/by Marcus Schneck.
                p.   cm.
      "A Fireside book."
      Includes index.
      ISBN 0-671-89246-0
      1. Butterfly gardening. I. Title.
QL644.6.S36   1994   93-39582
635.9'6--dc20.   CIP

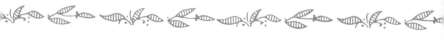

CONTENTS

GARDEN BUTTERFLY CONSERVATION

 ould there be a more mystical way to spend a gentle summer's afternoon than lolling on a bed of grassy carpet among a jungle of flowering plants and watching wispy wings of bright color flit above us? This spot could be your backyard butterfly garden.

Many butterfly species are easily attracted to our gardens. We have been luring these creatures for years with our traditional flower beds, often without a passing thought of the visitors that would eventually bring added coloring

to the results of our labors.

When we set out to design our gardens with butterflies in mind, filling them with plants and flowers that will attract and nurture the insects, the results can be spectacular. There are generally dozens of species in nearly every region of the continent that will respond, bringing with them a variety of color that is matched by no other group of wildlife.

Today across much of North America, the backyard and the garden are the dominant habitat types.

Whether intended or not, people are the determining factor in what's available to much wildlife, butterflies and others. We are now an important element in the conservation of many species.

Humankind's legacy to the butterfly has largely been one of destruction and devastation. Most species are intensely tied to their environments and cannot withstand our ever-growing pressures of development and land consumption.

◀ *The cabbage white, probably the most common butterfly species in North America, was introduced from Europe into Quebec in 1860.*

However, in recent years, we have been increasing the space devoted to our gardens, and even specifically to backyard wildlife habitats. In some urban, drought or otherwise inhospitable environments, our gardens help to maintain the local butterfly populations. Some species, such as the more common swallowtails, seem to have responded recently with some very strong population years.

One of the most important conservation decisions we can make concerns the use of pesticides, which should be avoided in the butterfly garden. Most of these chemicals are non-selective in the insects that they destroy, be they pests or desirable species like the butterflies. Even some "organic" pest-control methods have been found to be harmful to butterflies.

STAGES OF LIFE

Butterflies pass through an amazing transformation on their way to becoming what we commonly identify with that name. The process, known as metamorphosis, takes the insect from the egg through the caterpillar and chrysalis stages to the adult, winged butterfly.

Many butterfly species rely on different plant species during their two "eating" stages: food plants (usually the leaves) during the caterpillar stage and nectar plants during the adult stage. Some species will eat only one plant species and a few species do not eat during their adult stages. But these are definitely in the minority. Most have at least a short list of suitable plants.

A fully functioning butterfly garden that supports and maintains a population of butterflies from spring through early fall will include plants for both stages of life.

Adult (butterfly)

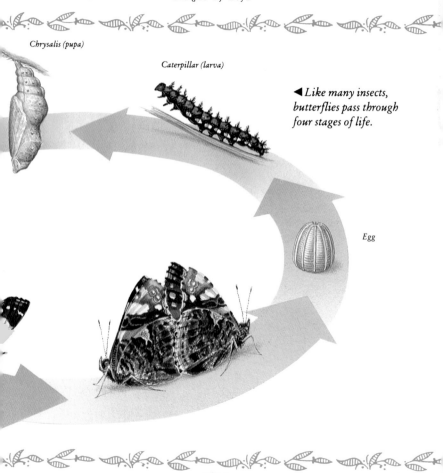

Chrysalis (pupa)

Caterpillar (larva)

◀ *Like many insects, butterflies pass through four stages of life.*

Egg

NECTAR AND FOOD PLANTS

ALFALFA *Medicago sativa*
nectar source Eastern Black Swallowtail, Orange Sulphur

APPLE *Malus* spp.
food plant – Spring Azure, Viceroy

ASTER *Aster* spp.
nectar source Checkered White, Common Sulphur, Orange Sulphur, Question Mark, American Painted Lady, Painted Lady, Red Admiral, Buckeye, Common Checkered Skipper, Fiery Skipper

BEANS *Phaseolus* spp.
food plant Gray Hairstreak, Silver-spotted Skipper

BEGGAR-TICKS *Bidens* spp.
nectar source Gulf Fritillary, Red Admiral, Monarch, Common Checkered Skipper, Fiery Skipper

BLACK-EYED SUSAN
Rudbeckia hirta
nectar source Great Spangled Fritillary

BUTTERFLY BUSH *Buddleia* spp.
nectar source Pipevine Swallowtail, Anise Swallowtail, Tiger Swallowtail Comma, American Painted Lady, Painted Lady, Monarch

BUTTONBUSH *Cephalanthus* spp.
nectar source Tiger Swallowtail, American Painted Lady, Painted Lady, Monarch

CARROT *Daucus carota*
food plant Eastern Black Swallowtail, Anise Swallowtail

DAISY *Chrysanthemum* spp.
nectar source Fiery Skipper

DANDELION *Taraxacum* spp.
nectar source Cabbage White, Common Sulphur, Comma

DOGBANE *Apocynum* spp.
nectar source Spicebush Swallowtail, Checkered White, Common Sulphur, Orange Sulphur, Gray Hairstreak, Spring Azure, American Painted Lady, Buckeye, Silver-spotted Skipper

DOGWOOD *Cornus* spp.
food plant Spring Azure
EVERLASTING *Anaphalis* spp.
Antennaria spp. *Gnaphalium* spp.
food plant American Painted Lady,
Painted Lady
FALSE FOXGLOVE
Aureolaria pedicularia
food plant Buckeye
GOLDENROD *Solidago* spp.
nectar source Common Sulphur,
Orange Sulphur, Gray Hairstreak,
American Painted Lady, Red Admiral

HOLLYHOCK *Alcea* spp.
food plant Painted Lady, Common
Checkered Skipper
IRONWEED *Vernonia* spp.
food plant American Painted Lady
nectar source Tiger Swallowtail, Great
Spangled Fritillary, Monarch, Fiery
Skipper
KNAPWEED *Centaurea* spp.
food plant Painted Lady
nectar source Common Sulphur,
American Painted Lady, Common
Checkered Skipper, Fiery Skipper
LANTANA *Lantana* spp.
nectar source Anise Swallowtail,
Spicebush Swallowtail, Cabbage White,
Gulf Fritillary, Fiery Skipper
MALLOW *Malva* spp.
food plant Gray Hairstreak,
Painted Lady
nectar source American Painted Lady,
Painted Lady, Red Admiral, Monarch

Apple

MILKWEED *Asclepias* spp.
food plant Monarch
nectar source Pipevine Swallowtail, Eastern Black Swallowtail, Giant Swallowtail, Tiger Swallowtail, Western Tiger Swallowtail, Spicebush Swallowtail, Checkered White, Cabbage White, Common Sulphur, Orange Sulphur, Gray Hairstreak, Spring Azure, Great Spangled Fritillary, Question Mark, American Painted Lady, Painted Lady, Red Admiral, Monarch, Fiery Skipper

Passion flower

MINT *Mentha* spp.
nectar source Western Black Swallowtail, Anise Swallowtail, Western Tiger Swallowtail, Cabbage White, Gray Hairstreak, American Painted Lady, Painted Lady, Red Admiral, Monarch
PARSLEY *Petroselinum crispum*
food plant Eastern Black Swallowtail, Anise Swallowtail
PASSION FLOWER *Passiflora* spp.
food plant Gulf Fritillary
nectar source Gulf Fritillary
PRIVET *Ligustrum* spp.
nectar source Spring Azure, American Painted Lady, Painted Lady, Silver-spotted Skipper
PURPLE CONEFLOWER *Echinacea* spp.
nectar source Great Spangled Fritillary
QUEEN-ANNE'S-LACE *Daucus carota var. carota*
food plant Eastern Black Swallowtail
nectar source Eastern Black Swallowtail, Gray Hairstreak

RED CLOVER *Trifolium pratense*
nectar source Cabbage White, Great
Spangled Fritillary, American Painted
Lady, Painted Lady, Red Admiral,
Silver-spotted Skipper, Common
Checkered Skipper
SELF-HEAL *Prunella* spp.
nectar source Cabbage White,
American Painted Lady, Silver-
spotted Skipper
SWEET PEA *Lathyrus odoratus*
food source Gray Hairstreak
nectar source Gray Hairstreak
THISTLE *Cirsium* spp.
food source Painted Lady
nectar source Pipevine Swallowtail,
Tiger Swallowtail, Western Tiger
Swallowtail, Spicebush Swallowtail,
Gulf Fritillary, Pearly Crescentspot,
American Painted Lady, Red Admiral,
Monarch, Silver-spotted Skipper
TICKSEED *Coreopsis grandiflora*
nectar source Common Sulphur,
Orange Sulphur, Buckeye, Monarch

VERBENA *Verbena* spp.
nectar source Great Spangled Fritillary
VETCH *Vicia* spp.
food plant Common Sulphur, Orange
Sulphur, Gray Hairstreak
nectar source American Painted Lady
VIOLET *Viola* spp.
food plant Great Spangled Fritillary
nectar source Spring Azure
WILLOW *Salix* spp.
food plant Tiger Swallowtail, Western
Tiger Swallowtail
WINTER CRESS *Barbarea* spp.
food plant Checkered White, Cabbage
White, Spring Azure
nectar source Checkered White, Gray
Hairstreak, Spring Azure, Silver-spotted
Skipper
WOOD NETTLE *Laportea canadensis*
food plant Comma, Red Admiral
WORMWOOD *Artemisia* spp.
food plant American Painted Lady
nectar source Tiger Swallowtail, Great
Spangled Fritillary, Monarch

PLANTS AS SHELTER

A relatively small number of North American butterfly species pass through the winter in their adult stage. But for those that do, and as added assistance to those that still frequent the garden during the fall, shelter can be provided in the form of log piles or a pile of leaf litter not removed from the corner of the garden during fall clean-up, or in a butterfly hibernation box.

A hibernation box is like a tall, thin, wooden birdbox. A minimum dimension is 3 feet tall by 6 inches wide by 6 inches deep. In place of the normally round hole of the birdbox, two 2-foot-long by 3/4-inch-wide slits should be cut into the front of the box. The structure should be mounted to a tree or post, or some similar upright in a location that is well-sheltered from the cold winds of winter.

◀ *Butterfly hibernation boxes are now available commercially through garden centers and nature stores. Key elements of these boxes are thin slit-type entrances and interior perching areas, such as bark strips.*

▶ *The monarch has responded to backyard butterfly gardens by expanding its range, but populations depend upon weather conditions in its Mexican wintering range.*

WATER AND PUDDLING

F ew butterfly species take advantage of what most other creatures would view as water sources. However, where moisture has soaked into the soil or sand leaving mud or a damp area, several species of butterfly will be quick to congregate.

The activity, which might find two dozen or more butterflies gathered together, is known as puddling. However, it appears that the minerals which the evaporating water releases to the soil surface are just as important to the insects as the moisture itself.

Some of the species most prone to puddling in significant numbers are the admirals, anglewings, fritillaries, hackberries, painted ladies, satyrs, skippers and swallowtails.

Studies at these sites have found that most of the butterflies gathered there are males and that sodium, which

is important to the males during the mating period, has the most drawing power of the minerals made available through this leaching process.

Sodium is a central component of salt, and the smaller salt blocks sold primarily for luring deer, elk and similar large mammals or for use in the live-stock industry can be installed in the butterfly garden as sort of a butterfly salt lick. It will be used regularly.

◀ *Most of the swallowtail species, such as this group of tiger swallowtails, are generally eager "puddlers," gathering in numbers wherever they find damp soils or drying mud puddles.*

THE GARDEN PLAN

Flowers blooming in abundance and over relatively large areas lend an added dimension of butterfly-attraction to the garden. The larger the flowering area and the more blooms appearing in it, the greater the number of butterflies that will be attracted.

In addition, you will want to extend the blooming season of your garden as early into the spring and as late into the fall as possible. To do this, plant a good mixture of annuals, which tend to bloom throughout the summer but must be replanted each year, and perennials, which bloom over more limited periods, but reappear yearly after the original planting.

Further, if you want to maximize the butterfly population making appearances in your garden, you must take the food plants of the caterpillars – often different from the nectar plants of the adults – into consideration as well. As butterflies which are native to this continent have evolved over time with the plants of North America, many of the best caterpillar food plants are native species.

Some of these, such as the butterfly bush and butterfly weed, are suitable for the traditional backyard garden. However, many have a "weed" appearance and would not be welcomed by many gardeners. A compromise often finds the "weeds" and native grasses planted in a plot near to, but separate from, flower beds.

▶ *Careful consideration of what your garden already holds is the first step in planning what you want it to become.*

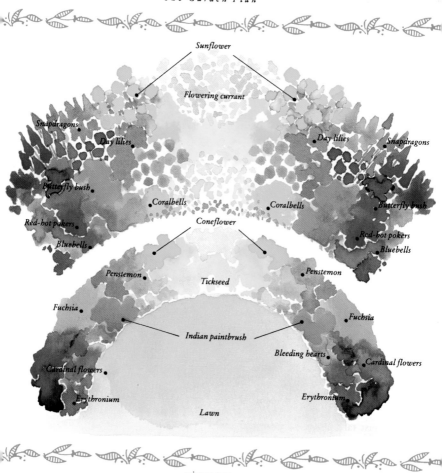

Sunflower

Flowering currant

Snapdragons

Day lilies

Day lilies

Snapdragons

Butterfly bush

Coralbells

Coralbells

Butterfly bush

Red-hot pokers

Coneflower

Red-hot pokers

Bluebells

Bluebells

Penstemon

Tickseed

Penstemon

Fuchsia

Fuchsia

Indian paintbrush

Bleeding hearts

Cardinal flowers

Cardinal flowers

Erythronium

Erythronium

Lawn

GARDEN PLAN

1 *House*
2 *Sliding patio doors*
3 *Patio*
4 *Existing ornamental shrubs*
5 *Stone walkway*
6 *Existing ornamental flower beds*
7 *Honeysuckle*
8 *Butterfly feeder*
9 *Island of butterfly flowers – verbena, lantana, butterfly weed, coreopsis*

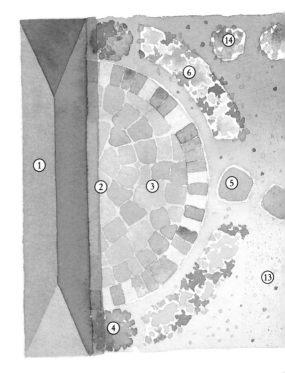

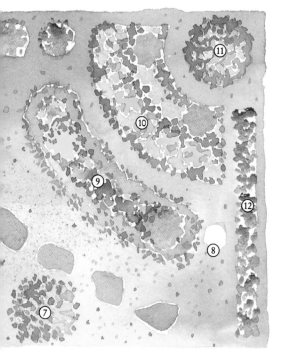

10 *Butterfly flower bed –
heliotrope, petunia,
nicotiana, butterfly
weed, coreopsis,
yarrow, bee balm,
black-eyed Susan,
purple coneflower*
11 *Cherry tree*
12 *Trellis with clematis*
13 *Open lawn*
14 *Butterfly bush*

LAYERING IN THE GARDEN

For a moment, try to put yourself into the wings of the butterfly. You need to feed on nectar throughout the day in order to survive. You need to draw that nectar from flowers that offer openings for your over-sized wings. And, while you are feeding, you are constantly vulnerable to attack, primarily from other winged creatures.

Obviously you are going to be attracted to flowers that not only grow in abundant clusters, but also allow for easy access. You won't want to fly down very far among the flowers because that would limit your escape options.

Layering provides all of these criteria. From the shorter plants in the front to the taller species in the rear, all the blossoms are readily available. Fortunately this layout also provides optimum viewing enjoyment.

◄ *The butterfly garden need not be a tangled meadow of wildflowers. Many of our ornamental flowers are attractive to butterflies. Layering flowers from the shortest in the front to the tallest in the rear, whether ornamentals or wild flowers, will present a more inviting setting.*

CREATING GARDEN ISLANDS

Just as islands in the ocean provide a sense of excitement for the approaching traveler, islands in the garden add accent to the plot's overall design.

Garden island design requires a more three-dimensional view of the property than traditional row, bed or edge gardening. All sides of the garden island will be seen. The impact of the island's placement and position on sunlight reaching the plants must be considered.

Layering, as discussed on pages 22-3, adds a great deal to a garden island. Again considering the three-dimensional aspect of the garden island, the chosen plants should be placed to build up from shorter species at the edge to taller species at the center from all sides of the island. The ultimate goal is to create a mound-like setting.

Circles and oblongs are the shapes that most gardeners seem to employ when they first begin experimenting with islands. However, crescents, zigzags and similarly unusual shapes further enhance the mystique that garden islands begin to create. Pathways can be laid out between and among the islands to create a maze or honeycomb effect and the setting for many pleasant sojourns.

▶ *Islands, whether spread throughout the garden or used as garden borders, offer greater flower-surface area and access for our butterfly visitors. This is a benefit to the gardener as islands present a more interesting design element than large bed areas of flowers.*

VINES, SHRUBS, AND TREES

We tend to think immediately of flower beds when we begin discussing gardens for butterflies. Our initial plans often travel no higher than our waists.

On the other hand, in their adult stage, butterflies are very much creatures of the air, and few blossom-producing plants that we can grow in our gardens will go unnoticed by our insect diners. Fruit orchards, at least those that have not been too heavily drenched in pesticides, provide amazing testimony to this fact with their droves of flitting butterflies during the blossom season.

Several common garden shrub and vine species are also particularly attractive to butterflies. Among them are the various buddleia species (particularly butterfly bush), caryopteris, lilac, spicebush and wisteria.

▲ *Flowering shrubs, such as this wisteria, vines and trees can provide additional options in the butterfly garden.*

▲ *A monarch butterfly takes nectar from the flowers of a butterfly bush, one of the most attractive plants for the insects.*

THE SPRING GARDEN

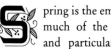 pring is the emerging time for much of the natural world, and particularly for certain families such as butterflies. Early spring will be greeted by such common species as the cabbage white, and perhaps by a few false starts for other species when unseasonally warm temperatures appear and disappear from day to day. Gradually, however, those warmer temperatures become the standard, and the variety of butterfly color in the garden begins to increase.

All through the spring, this gradual emergence continues. Some species have spent the winter in adult form and await the warming of their cracks and crevices where they dwell before making an appearance. Others have passed the colder months as eggs or chrysalides, and must now emerge and grow into their winged, adult versions. Still others migrated south for the winter – notably the Monarch – and they, or their progeny, are now returning north.

Your plants respond to the increasing warmth and sunlight in much the same way, adding to the growing color of the garden. Each day, now, seems to bring change. A new bud here, a bud opening into full flower there, or a new butterfly species making an unexpected visit to the garden.

▶ *Buds, then flowers, gradually appear throughout the spring. And with them come the butterflies. Some flowers, particularly those of many trees, will only benefit these early visitors.*

SPRING GARDEN
1 *Arabis*
2 *Aubretia*
3 *Rhododendron*
4 *Red buckeye*
5 *Dame's rocket*
6 *Lilac*
7 *Allium*

SPRING PLANTS

ARABIS
Arabis albida
Grows to 1½ feet
Perennial
Zone 5 south
Various soil types
Full sun

Rhododendron

AUBRIETA
Aubrieta deltoidea
Grows to 1 foot
Perennial
Zone 4 south
Well-drained soil
Full sun

RHODODENDRON
Rhododendron spp.
Grows to 7 feet
Evergreen
Zone 4 south
Acidic soil
Partial sun

RED BUCKEYE
Aesculus pavia
Grows to 18 feet
Semi-evergreen
Zone 5 south
Various soil conditions
Partial sun

DAME'S ROCKET
Hesperis matronalis
Grows to 3 feet
Perennial
Moist soil
Full sun

LILAC
Syringa vulgaris
Grows to 12 feet
Partially evergreen
Zone 5 south
Clayey soil
Full sun

ALLIUM
Allium spp.
Grows to 1 foot
Perennial
Zone 5 south
Various soil types
Full sun

LUNARIA
Lunaria annua
Grows to 2 feet
Biennial
Zone 5 south
Various soil types
Full sun

FORGET-ME-NOT
Myosotis sylvatica
Grows to 1 foot
Perennial
Zone 4 south
Slightly acidic soil
Partial sun

CHIVES
Allium schoenoprasm
Grows to 1 foot
Perennial
Zone 4 south
Well-drained, fertile soil
Full sun

CHERRY
Prunus spp.
Grows to 80 feet
Deciduous
All zones
Various soil conditions
Full sun

WILLOW
Salix spp.
Grows to 30 feet
Deciduous
Zone 5 south
Moist soil
Full sun

JAPANESE HONEYSUCKLE
Lonicera japonica
Grows to 30 feet
Semi-evergreen
Zone 5 south
Cool, moist soil
Partial sun

Forget-me-not

FEEDERS AND RECIPES

Butterflies will quickly adopt homemade feeders as part of their daily routines, and you can take a measure of pride in the fact that you have added something to the natural landscape that wild creatures have accepted as belonging there.

An inverted jar or bottle – any size will do, but nothing larger than a baby food jar really is necessary – with a small hole drilled in the center of the lid and some cotton plugged into that hole, is an easily created feeder. Fill the bottle with

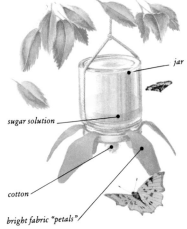

jar

sugar solution

cotton

bright fabric "petals"

sugar solution. The cotton absorbs the "nectar" and the butterfly "feeds" on the cotton. Cutting some brightly colored fabrics and placing them around the cotton to resemble the petals of a flower adds considerably to the feeder's attraction for butterflies, who do much nectar-spotting by sight.

An even simpler feeder, which will attract many species of butterflies, can be made by pouring the food solution onto an open area of soil or sand, or into a shallow dish filled with sand, near the flower beds.

Food solution is a similarly simple matter for butterflies. Sugar dissolved in water, at no more than one part to nine parts respectively, has proven to be an effective recipe. No coloring needs to be added. You can use any kind of sugar, but not honey or other sweeteners,

In addition to such sugar – water feeders, some butterfly species also will feed on rotting fruit and oozing tree sap. Such fruit can be placed near the flower beds as another feeder.

◀ ▶ *Butterfly feeders are a relatively new fixture for gardeners. However, they are becoming more readily available through nurseries and garden centers. Homemade versions, as shown at left, can be easy to make, inexpensive, and easy to maintain.*

THE SUMMER GARDEN

Summer is truly prime time in the butterfly garden. For the successful gardener, more plants are now in bloom than at any other time of the year. The butterflies, of many sizes and colors, are responding to all those sources of nectar. Color is everywhere.

It's time to sit back with an iced tea or lemonade and enjoy the fruits of our labors. Unfortunately, it's also the season of maximum pest insect activity in the garden, so our respite is often interrupted. The urge to turn to pesticides can be almost unbearable at times. Quick response to the beginnings of any pest problems that are spotted are much preferred to the use of chemicals; it can often be as simple as removing the problem insects physically. If discovered early most infestations can be headed off.

◀ *Flowers bloom in great profusion in the summer garden. This is the height of the flowering season, and all through this period more and more butterflies – both in numbers and variety – will be making regular visits for nectar.*

SUMMER GARDEN

1 *Ageratum*
2 *Heliotrope*
3 *Lantana*
4 *Scabiosa*
5 *Butterfly weed*
6 *Coreopsis*
7 *Lavender*
8 *Bee balm*

9 *Black-eyed Susan*
10 *Lily*
11 *Loosestrife*
12 *Phlox*
13 *Purple coneflower*
14 *Butterfly bush*
15 *Honeysuckle*

SUMMER PLANTS

Ageratum

AGERATUM
Ageratum houstonianum
Grows to 1½ feet
Annual
All regions
Moist soil
Full sun

HELIOTROPE
Heliotropium arborescens
Grows to 2 feet
Annual
Zone 5 south
Rich soil
Full sun

LANTANA
Lantana camara
Grows to 10 feet
Evergreen from Zone 8
south; annual between
Zones 4 and 8
Rich, well-composted
soil
Full sun

SCABIOSA
Scabiosa atropurpurea
Grows to 1 foot
Perennial or annual
All regions
Well-drained soil
Full sun

BUTTERFLY WEED*
Flowers from May to
September

COREOPSIS
Coreopsis spp.
Grows to 2 feet
Perennial or annual
All zones
Well-drained soil
Full sun

LAVENDER
Lavandula angustifolia
Grows to 4 feet
Evergreen
Zone 8 south
Well-drained soil
Full sun

BEE BALM
Monarda didyma
Grows to 4 feet
Perennial
Zone 3 south
Moist soil
Full sun

BLACK-EYED SUSAN
Rudbekia hirta
Grows to 3 feet
Perennial or biennial
All zones
Various soil types
Full sun

LILY
Lilium spp.
Grows to 6 feet
Perennial
All zones
Moist, well-mulched soil
Partial sun

LOOSESTRIFE
Lythrum virgatum
Grows to 5 feet
Perennial
All zones
Moist soil
Full sun

PHLOX
Phlox spp.
Grows to 3 feet
Perennial or annual
All zones
Moist soil
Full sun

PURPLE CONEFLOWER
Echinacea purpurea
Grows to 1½ feet
Perennial
Zone 3 south
Well-drained soil
Full sun

BUTTERFLY BUSH
Buddleia davidii
Grows to 10 feet
Semi-evergreen
Zone 5 south
Alkaline soil
Full sun

HONEYSUCKLE
Lonicera tatarica
Grows to 7 feet
Evergreen or
semi-evergreen
Zone 3 south
Well-drained soil
Full or partial sun

Lavender

* For gardening facts,
see pages 54-5

SUNLIGHT AND SHELTER

Butterflies need sunlight almost as much as they need the right nectar and food plants. Only when their body temperatures are above 85° Fahrenheit can they take full advantage of their flight abilities.

And, like cold-blooded creatures, they rely on the sun for their heat. Basking is thus a crucial part of butterfly life. For this reason we generally see less butterfly activity in the morning and on cloudy days.

A sun-filled garden, where nearly all of the day's sunlight reaches the flowering plants, provides many benefits for the butterflies. They can begin flying and feeding earlier in the day and continue later in the day. They have more time to mate and lay more eggs. Also, eggs and caterpillars in sunny locations have shown increased growth rates.

In addition, flowers generally produce more nectar and food plants more green growth in sunny spots. Such abundance can support more butterflies.

Locations that are sunny *and* sheltered from the wind are even more attractive to both butterflies and plants. For the insects, shelter means they do not lose body temperature to the wind and they do not need to struggle against wind while in flight. For the plants, shelter means extended blooming season, both earlier in the spring and later in the fall.

Such shelter is easily provided with a row of shrubs or trees, a fence, or wall. However, the sheltering device needs to be positioned so that while it blocks much of the wind, it doesn't screen out too much of the day's sunlight, which warms the insects.

◀ *Shelter areas in close
proximity to the flower
beds, such as the hedge at
left and the trees in the
background, provide an
ideal setting to attract
butterflies. The shelter
areas provide resting
cover for the butterflies
and take the force out
of winds.*

THE EARLY FALL GARDEN

As fall approaches our butterfly visitors begin to disappear. Some are now "sleeping" as eggs or chrysalides, waiting for the coming warmth of next spring. Others have begun their annual migration to the warmer climates of the south.

Our flowers, too, are disappearing. More color seems to leave the garden every day. And we've begun the task of cleaning up the garden for the winter. There are dying plants to be composted. There are leaves to be raked.

Now is the time to tread carefully in just how much clean-up we do. Some of our summertime guests have already set up housekeeping in those piles of leaves that have collected along the hedge or among those wood piles at the rear of the garden. Perhaps there are a few spots where we can allow a bit of winter sanctuary to remain.

◀ *Careful selection of flower types can achieve many different goals in the garden. Some, such as these marigolds, have extremely long-lasting flowering periods. They'll provide garden color and butterfly attraction throughout the summer months, and well into fall in many zones.*

EARLY FALL GARDEN

1 *Sweet pepperbush*
2 *Verbena*
3 *Sneezeweed*
4 *Nicotiana*
5 *Cosmos*
6 *Zinnia*
7 *Globe thistle*
8 *Obedient plant*
9 *Sedum*
10 *Willow*
11 *Glossy abelia*
12 *Aster*
13 *Bluebeard*
14 *Cherry*
15 *Statice*

EARLY FALL PLANTS

SWEET PEPPERBUSH
Clenthra alnifolia
Grows to 9 feet
Perennial
Zone 3 south
Various soil conditions
Full sun

VERBENA
Verbena x hortensis
Grows to 2 feet
Perennial or annual
All regions
Well-drained soil
Full sun

SNEEZEWEED
Helenium autumnale
Grows to 4 feet
All zones
Perennial
Various soil conditions
Full sun

NICOTIANA
Nicotiana alata
Grows to 3 feet
Annual
Zone 5 south
Well-composted,
well-drained soil
Full sun

Nicotiana

COSMOS
Cosmos bipinnatus
Grows to 2 feet
Annual
All zones
Well-drained soil
Full sun

ZINNIA
Zinnia elegans
Grows to 3 feet
Annual
All regions
Well-drained soil
Full sun

GLOBE THISTLE
Echinops exaltatus
Grows to 4 feet
Zone 3 south
Perennial
Well-drained soil
Full sun

OBEDIENT PLANT
Physostegia virginiana
Grows to 3 feet
Zone 4 south
Perennial
Various soil conditions
Full sun

SEDUM
Sedum spectabile vulgaris
Grows to less than 1 foot
Perennial
Zone 3 south
Well-drained soil
Full sun

WILLOW*
Blossoms are gone, but
the hanging foliage
provides shelter
throughout much of
the fall

GLOSSY ABELIA
Abelia x grandiflora
Grows to 4 feet
Zone 4 south
Semi-evergreen
Various soil conditions
Full sun

ASTER
Aster spp.
Grows to 3 feet
Perennial
Zone 4 south
Moist soil
Full sun

BLUEBEARD
Caryopteris x clandonensis
Grows to 5 feet
All zones
Deciduous
Sandy soil
Full sun

CHERRY*
The leaves of hardwood
tree species, such as
cherry, provide excellent
mulching materials

STATICE
Limonium sinuatum
Grows to 2 feet
Perennial
Zone 4 south
Various soil conditions
Full sun

---

*For gardening facts,
see pages 32-3

A WILDFLOWER OPTION

Native plants, today commonly referred to as wildflowers and native grasses, are an important consideration for the butterfly garden. You can, of course, create a garden with nothing but domesticated plant species and still enjoy success in attracting butterflies. However, the addition of wildflowers and native grasses – those species with which the butterflies have evolved and developed over thousands of years – will bring a new aspect to the garden and enhance its attraction for the butterflies.

Some important native species are aster, beggar ticks, boneset, butterfly weed, dandelion, dogbane, goldenrod, hawkweed, ironweed, Joe-Pye weed, milkweed, mountain mint, oxeye daisy, pearly everlasting, Queen Anne's lace, thistle, vetch, white clover, wild bergamot, winter cress and yarrow.

You will notice that many of these plant species also would be found on many gardeners' lists of the most noxious and hated weeds in existence. Be that as it may – "weed" is a very subjective term – all of these are very attractive to butterflies.

▶ *Native plants, such as these Indian paintbrushes, are becoming much more commonly available. They hold a strong attraction for butterflies because they and the insects have evolved to complement one another over many generations.*

WILDFLOWER OPTION

1 *Dandelion*
2 *Clover*
3 *Butterfly weed*
4 *Dogbane*

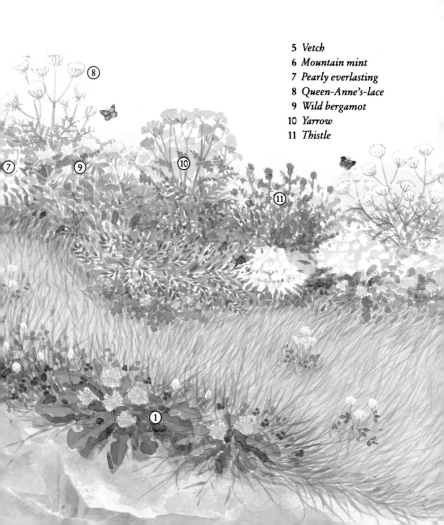

5 *Vetch*
6 *Mountain mint*
7 *Pearly everlasting*
8 *Queen-Anne's-lace*
9 *Wild bergamot*
10 *Yarrow*
11 *Thistle*

WILDFLOWERS

DANDELION
Taraxacum officinale
Grows to 1 foot
Perennial
All zones
Various soil conditions
Full sun

CLOVER
Trifolium spp.
Grows to 1 foot
Perennial
All zones
Various soil conditions
Full to partial sun

BUTTERFLY WEED
Asclepias tuberosa
Grows to 3 feet
Perennial
Zone 3 south
Well-drained soil
Full sun

DOGBANE
Apocynum androsaemifolium
Grows to ½ foot
Evergreen
Zone 5 south
Well-drained soil
Full sun

VETCH
Vicia americana
Grows to 4 feet
Perennial
Generally overwinters
very well in all zones
Well-drained soil
Sun-loving

MOUNTAIN MINT
Pycanthemum spp.
Grows to 3 feet
Perennial
Zone 3 south
Moist soil
Partial sun

Butterfly weed

PEARLY EVERLASTING
Anaphalis margaritacea
Grows to 1½ feet
Perennial
Zone 3 south
Well-drained soil
Partial sun

QUEEN-ANNE'S-LACE
Daucus carota var. *carota*
Grows to 2-3½ft
Biennial
Zone 2 south
Various soil conditions
Full sun

Wild bergamot

WILD BERGAMOT
Monarda fistulosa
Grows to 4 feet
Perennial
Zone 3 south
Well-drained soil
Full to partial sun

YARROW
Achillea millefolium
Grows to 4 feet
Perennial
All zones
Well-drained soil
Full sun

THISTLE
Cirsium spp.
Grows to 6 feet
Perennial
Care must be taken to contain this invasive plant's roots
Well-drained soil
Sun-loving

STOCKING BUTTERFLIES

A quick, albeit non-guaranteed, route to having butterflies in your garden is to stock them there yourself. Several small companies and individuals now operate in various parts of North America raising butterflies for various uses, including stocking in gardens. They

generally can recommend and deliver appropriate species for your region. However, they cannot promise that the butterfly won't leave your garden as soon as it emerges from the chrysalis.

The chrysalis is generally the easiest form in which to transport butterflies, so it is the form most widely used by commercial suppliers.

But for those gardeners who want to try to collect their own butterfly stock from the wild, eggs are probably the most convenient form. (Before attempting such collection and relocation, you should be familiar with all regulations that apply to your local area.) With a field guide that illustrates the eggs of some species common to your area, small plant shears or scissors, and a magnifying glass, head for the nearest patch of wild growth in your neighborhood.

When you find eggs that you can identify – usually on the underside of leaves or along the stems – clip that section of the plant and place it in some

protective, vented container with additional pieces of the plant leaves. Note the exact species of plant on which you found the eggs.

Place the eggs and leaf pieces in a large jar with a vented cap. When the eggs begin to hatch into caterpillars, fetch several stalks of the plant species on which they were found and place these in the jar (for the caterpillar to feed on), along with a twig leaning from the bottom to one side. Replace the plant parts daily until the caterpillar attaches itself to the twig and molts into the chrysalis.

Monitor the chrysalis regularly and the morning after an adult butterfly emerges release it into your garden.

◀ *A monarch perches on the chrysalis from which it emerged.*

BUTTERFLY SUPPLY HOUSES

These are just a few of the many companies that now offer butterfly lifecycle kits, complete with butterfly larvae, to the public:

American Science & Surplus, 601 Linden Place, Evanston, IL 60202

Connecticut Valley Biological Supply Co., P.O. Box 326, Southampton, MA 01073

Delta Education, Box M, Nashua, NH 03061-6012

Museum Products, 84 Rt. 27, Mystic, CT 06355

Papillon Distributors Inc., P.O. Box 1463, 26 Bedford St., Waltham, MA 02254

Southern Biological Supply Co., P.O. Box 68, McKenzie, TN 38201

Young Entomologists' Society Inc., 1915 Peggy Place, Lansing, MI 48910-2553

THE NIGHT GARDEN

At night our butterfly garden is visited by a whole new group of nectar-drinkers. Misunderstood, and often unnoticed because of their nocturnal habits, moths have not received the welcome given to their butterfly cousins.

Most often they have been seen only as dull-colored destroyers of our crops, our clothes and the like. However, it is only a small minority of the moth species in North America that account for most of the damage. The vast majority do us no harm. As a matter of fact, like other nectar-drinkers (such as butterflies), many moth species perform important pollination duties.

And, while it's true that many moth species are not as brightly colored as the day-flying butterflies, they all have their subtle shades and hues that give them a beauty of their own.

In addition, some are colorful enough to rival anything in the butterfly family. The nearly luminescent green of the luna moth's wings and the bright red of the cecropia moth's body are just two of the most common examples.

The same plants that attract butterflies during the day with their scents and nectars will attract moths during the night. The gardener interested in extending the wonders of the butterfly garden to the full 24-hour period might also consider adding a few low-standing, path-type lights, which will attract even more varieties of moths.

▶ *The cecropia moth is one of the larger, more colorful North American species.*

NIGHT GARDEN

1 *Petunia*
2 *Cosmos*
3 *Nicotiana*
4 *Candytuft*
5 *Daffodil*
6 *Delphinium*

COMMON BUTTERFLIES AND MOTHS

More than 1000 species of butterflies and moths can be found in North America, north of the U.S.-Mexico border. Some are so rare and occupy so limited a range that a great deal of time, effort, and travel would be necessary for most of us to view them in the wild. Some are only occasional visitors to small enclaves on the continent. But a third group is so common and widespread that many readers of this book can realistically expect to see at least some of them year-in-year-out. The following species have been selected from this latter group. Because of their daytime presence, butterflies are generally spotted more frequently. However, various moth species will generally be found in the same areas.

◀ *Although most butterflies are creatures of open fields and grasslands, like this orange sulphur they will regularly seek the shelter of trees.*

EASTERN BLACK SWALLOWTAIL
Papilio polyxenes

Range: All of U.S. and southern Canada east of the Rockies
Habitat: Open, weedy areas

PIPEVINE SWALLOWTAIL
Battus philenor

Range: All of U.S. east and south of the Rockies, southern Canada
Habitat: Open, weedy areas

ANISE SWALLOWTAIL
Papilio zelicaon

Range: U.S. and Canada west of the Rockies
Habitat: Wide ranging

GIANT SWALLOWTAIL
Heraclides cresphontes
Range: U.S. and southern Canada east and south of the Rockies
Habitat: Open, grassy areas near woodlots

TIGER SWALLOWTAIL
Pterourus glaucus

Range: Eastern half of the U.S., north and west through central Canada
Habitat: Wide ranging

SPICEBUSH SWALLOWTAIL
Pterourus troilus

Range: Eastern U.S. and southern Canada
Habitat: Wooded areas, fields, gardens

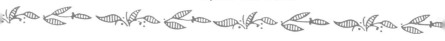

COMMON WHITE
Pontia protodice

Range: All U.S. except
Pacific Northwest
Habitat: Open, grassy
and weedy areas

ZEBRA
SWALLOWTAIL
Eurytides marcellus

Range: Eastern U.S. and
southern Canada
Habitat: Wooded areas
near water

CABBAGE WHITE
Pieris rapae

Range: All U.S. and all
but northernmost
Canada
Habitat: Cosmopolitan

ORANGE SULFUR
Colias eurytheme

Range: All U.S. and all but northernmost Canada
Habitat: Open, grassy areas

FALCATE ORANGETIP
Anthocharis midea

Range: Eastern half of the U.S. south to northern Florida and Texas
Habitat: Moist areas in forests

COMMON SULFUR
Colias philodice

Range: All U.S. except Florida, and all but northernmost Canada
Habitat: Open, grassy areas

DOGFACE BUTTERFLY
Zerene cesonia

Range: Southern half of the U.S. and north through the Great Plains
Habitat: Widespread

SLEEPY ORANGE
Eurema nicippe

Range: Southern U.S.
Habitat: Open, wooded and second-growth areas

GULF FRITILLARY
Agraulis vanillae

Range: All U.S. and southwestern Canada
Habitat: Open areas

GREAT SPANGLED FRITILLARY
Speyeria cybele

Range: All U.S. except southern third, and southern Canada
Habitat: Open, wooded areas

VARIEGATED FRITILLARY
Euptoieta claudia

Range: All U.S. and southern Canada
Habitat: Cosmopolitan, except for heavily wooded areas

APHRODITE
Speyeria aphrodite

Range: Northern half of the U.S. and southern half of Canada, west to the Rocky mountains
Habitat: Wooded areas

QUESTION MARK
Polygonia interrogationis

Range: U.S. and southern Canada east of the Rockies
Habitat: Wooded areas, but with openings

MEADOW FRITILLARY
Clossiana bellona

Range: Northern half of the U.S. and southern half of Canada
Habitat: Damp, weedy areas

COMMA
Polygonia comma

Range: Eastern half of the U.S. and Canada
Habitat: Surburban areas

<u>VICEROY</u>
Basilarchia archippus

Range: All but
westernmost U.S. and
southern Canada
Habitat: Damp areas

<u>AMERICAN</u>
<u>PAINTED LADY</u>
Vanessa virginiensis

Range: All U.S. and all
but northernmost
Canada
Habitat: Open, sunny
areas

<u>PAINTED LADY</u>
Vanessa cardui

Range: All U.S. and all
but northernmost
Canada
Habitat: Quite
cosmopolitan

AMERICAN COPPER
Lycaena phlaeas

Range: All but southern U.S. and northern Canada
Habitat: Open regrowth areas

EASTERN TAILED BLUE
Everes comyntas

Range: All U.S. and southern Canada
Habitat: Disturbed areas

SPRING AZURE
Celastrina ladon

Range: All U.S. and all but northern Canada
Habitat: Wooded areas and nearby open areas

NORTHERN HAIRSTREAK
Euristrymon ontario

Range: U.S. and southern Canada, west to Rocky Mountains
Habitat: Wooded areas

SILVERY BLUE
Glaucopsyche lygdamus

Range: All U.S. except southernmost, and all Canada except northernmost
Habitat: Widespread

GRAY HAIRSTREAK
Strymon melinus

Range: All U.S. and southern Canada
Habitat: Cosmopolitan

MONARCH
Danaus plexippus

Range: All U.S. and
Canada, except Pacific
Northwest
Habitat: Cosmopolitan

BUCKEYE
Junonia coenia

Range: U.S. and southern
Canada east of the
Rockies; also U.S. Pacific
Northwest
Habitat: Open, weedy
areas

SILVER-SPOTTED
SKIPPER
Epargyreus clarus

Range: All U.S. and all
but northern Canada
Habitat: Open wooded
and grassy areas

COMMON CHECKERED SKIPPER
Pholisoria catullus

Range: All U.S. and all but northern Canada
Habitat: Open, weedy areas

LEAST SKIPPERLING
Ancyloxypha numitor

Range: Eastern half of the U.S. and southern Canada
Habitat: Near moist agricultural areas

FIERY SKIPPER
Hylephila phyleus

Range: Northeastern U.S., south and west to southern California
Habitat: Open, grassy areas

<u>SACHEM</u>
Atalopedes campestris

Range: Southern half of the U.S.
Habitat: Open, grassy and weedy areas

<u>NORTHERN BROKEN DASH</u>
Wallengrenia egeremet

Range: Eastern half of U.S. and Canada
Habitat: Shrubs and fields

<u>DUN SKIPPER</u>
Euphyes ruricola

Range: All U.S. and southern Canada
Habitat: Widespread

<u>RED ADMIRAL</u>
Vanessa atalanta

Range: All U.S. and all but northernmost Canada
Habitat: Open areas

HUMMINGBIRD MOTH
Hemaris thysbe

Range: All northern U.S. and southern Canada, also west to the Great Plains in the southern U.S.
Habitat: Widespread

WHITE-LINED SPHINX
Hyles lineata

Range: All U.S. and southern Canada
Habitat: Widespread

VIRGINIA CREEPER SPHINX
Darapsa myron

Range: Eastern half of U.S. and southeastern Canada
Habitat: Always near wooded, shrubby areas

PANDORA SPHINX
Eumorpha pandorus

Range: Eastern half of
U.S. and southeastern
Canada
Habitat: Wooded areas
and along waterways

LUNA MOTH
Actias luna

Range: Eastern U.S. and
southern Canada
Habitat: Near deciduous
woodlands

IMPERIAL MOTH
Eacles imperialis

Range: U.S. and southern
Canada, west to the
Rocky Mountains
Habitat: Wooded areas

IO MOTH
Automeris io

Range: U.S. and southern
Canada, west to the
Rocky Mountains
Habitat: Grassy, weedy
and wooded areas

CECROPIA MOTH
Hyalophora cecropia

Range: U.S. and southern
Canada, west to the
Rocky Mountains
Habitat: Widespread in
open, grassy areas

PROMETHEA MOTH
Callosamia promethea

Range: Eastern half of
U.S. and southern
Canada
Habitat: Widespread

INDEX

ACKNOWLEDGMENTS

All images in this book are the
copyright of Quarto Publishing Inc.
except for the following:
Diane Calkins *36*; Photo/Nats *6, 26*;
Unicorn Stock Photos *15, 23-4, 25, 26,
27, 29, 35, 43, 45, 51, 56, 59, 62.*